Math in Focus™

The Singapore Approach

Student Book
Kindergarten Ⓑ
Part 2

Author
Dr. Pamela Sharpe

U.S. Consultants
Andy Clark and Patsy F. Kanter

Marshall Cavendish
Education

GREAT SOURCE®
HOUGHTON MIFFLIN HARCOURT
Supplemental Publishers

© 2009 Marshall Cavendish International (Singapore) Private Limited

Published by Marshall Cavendish Education
An imprint of Marshall Cavendish International (Singapore) Private Limited
A member of Times Publishing Limited

Marshall Cavendish International (Singapore) Private Limited
Times Centre, 1 New Industrial Road
Singapore 536196
Tel: +65 6411 0820
Fax: +65 6266 3677
E-mail: fps@sg.marshallcavendish.com
Website: www.marshallcavendish.com/education/sg

Distributed by
Great Source
A division of Houghton Mifflin Harcourt Publishing Company
181 Ballardvale Street
P.O. Box 7050
Wilmington, MA 01887-7050
Tel: 1-800-289-4490
Website: www.greatsource.com

First published 2009

Math in Focus ™ is a trademark of Marshall Cavendish Education.

Great Source ® is a registered trademark of Houghton Mifflin Harcourt Publishing Company.

Math in Focus Kindergarten B Part 2
ISBN 978-0-669-01638-3

Printed in Singapore

1 2 3 4 5 6 7 8 MCI 16 15 14 13 12 11 10 09 08

Contents

Chapter 15 Length and Height

Lesson 1 'Long' and 'Short'

Draw a long tail.

Draw a short tail.

Make an X on the kite with the longest tail.
Circle the kite with the shortest tail.

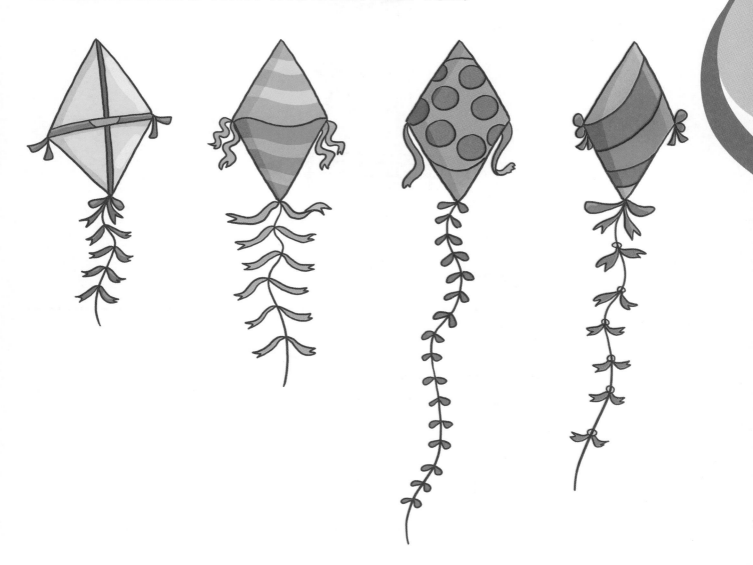

Lesson 3 Comparing Lengths Using Non-standard Units

Measure, count and write.

The pencil is _____ cubes long.

The spoon is _____ cubes long.

The toothbrush is _____ cubes long.

The comb is _____ cubes long.

The tube is _____ cubes long.

The paint brush is _____ cubes long.

Comparing Heights Using Non-standard Units

Count and write. Make an X on the taller vase.

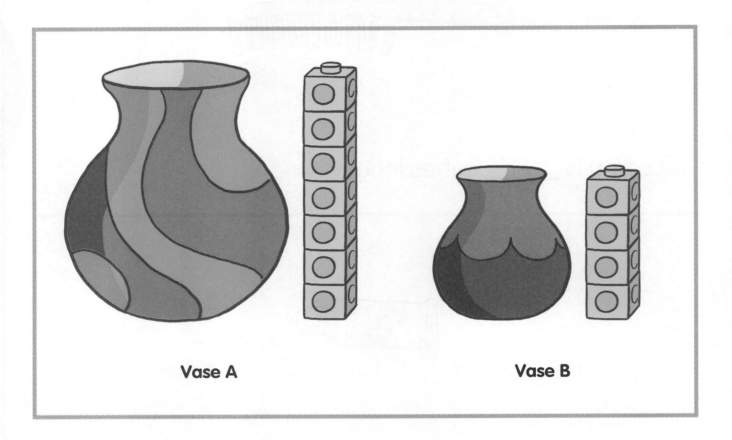

Vase A

Vase B

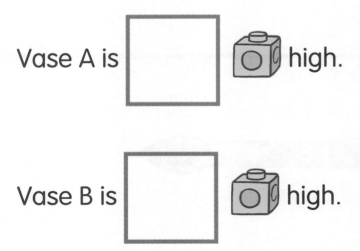

Vase A is [ ] high.

Vase B is [ ] high.

Count and write. Circle the shorter flower.

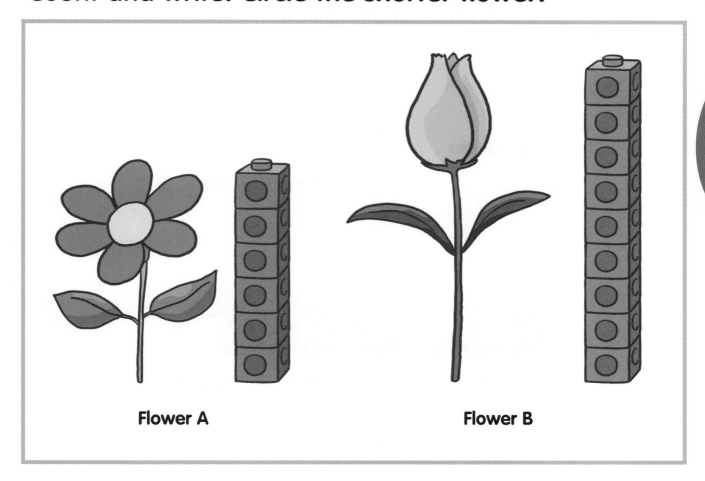

Flower A　　　　　　　　　**Flower B**

Flower A is ☐ 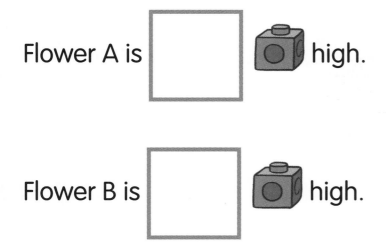 high.

Flower B is ☐ high.

Lesson 5 Finding Differences in Length Using Non-standard Units

Count and write.

The caterpillar is 3 🖇 longer than the ant.

The pencil is _____ 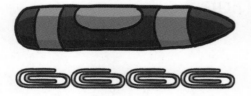 long.

The crayon is _____ 🖇 long.

The pencil is _____ 🖇 longer than the crayon.

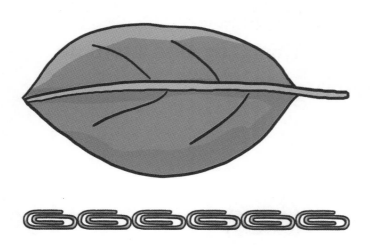

The leaf is _____ 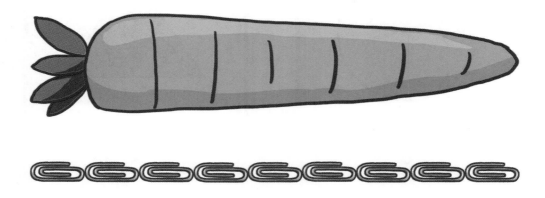 long.

The carrot is _____ long.

The leaf is _____ shorter than the carrot.

Chapter 16 Classifying and Sorting

Lesson 1 Classifying Things by One Attribute

Sort and match.

 •

 •

 •

•

•

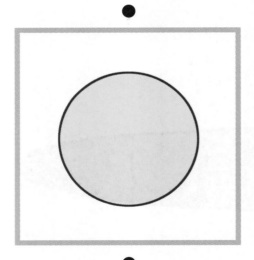

•

•

•

•

•

10

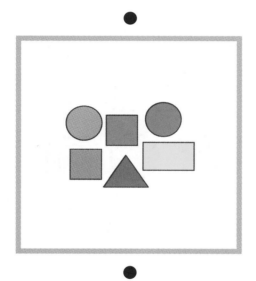

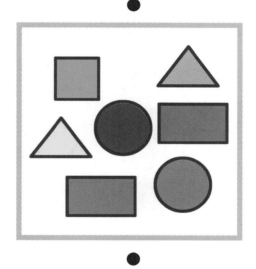

Sort and match.

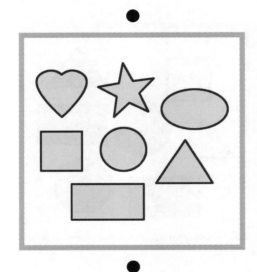

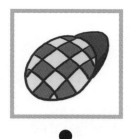

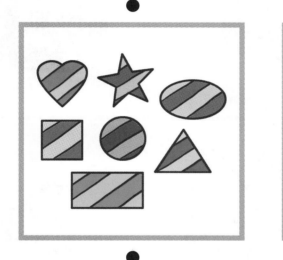

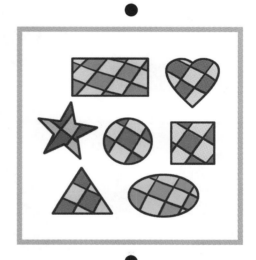

Make an X on the item that does not belong.

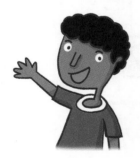  

  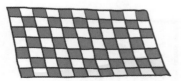

Chapter 17

Addition Stories

Lesson 1 Writing Addition Sentences

Count and write.

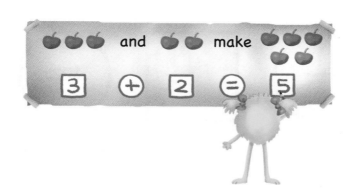

 and  make

| 4 | + | 3 | = | |

 and  make

| 2 | + | | = | |

Count and write.

 and  make

 +  =

 and  make

 ○  ○

 and  make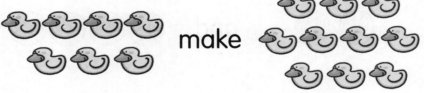

 ○  ○

Count and write.

Count and write.

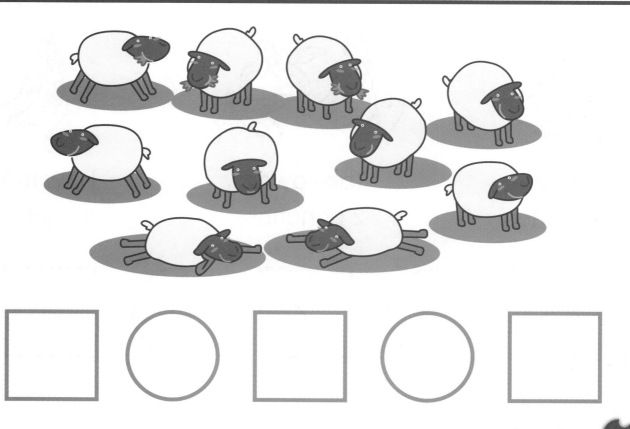

Chapter 18

Subtraction Stories

Lesson 1 Writing Subtraction Sentences

Count and write.

There are
4 ducks.

Take away
2 ducks.

How many
are left?

4 ⊖ 2 = 2

There are
5 bananas.

Take away
2 bananas.

How many
are left?

 ⊖  ⊜

5 — 2 =

There are
7 candles.

Take away
3 candles.

How many
are left?

  −   =

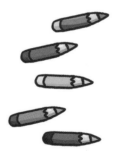

There are
9 pencils.

Take away
4 pencils.

How many
are left?

Lesson 2 Showing Subtraction Stories with Numbers

Count and write.

Lesson 3 Comparing Sets

How many more? Circle. Write the number sentence.

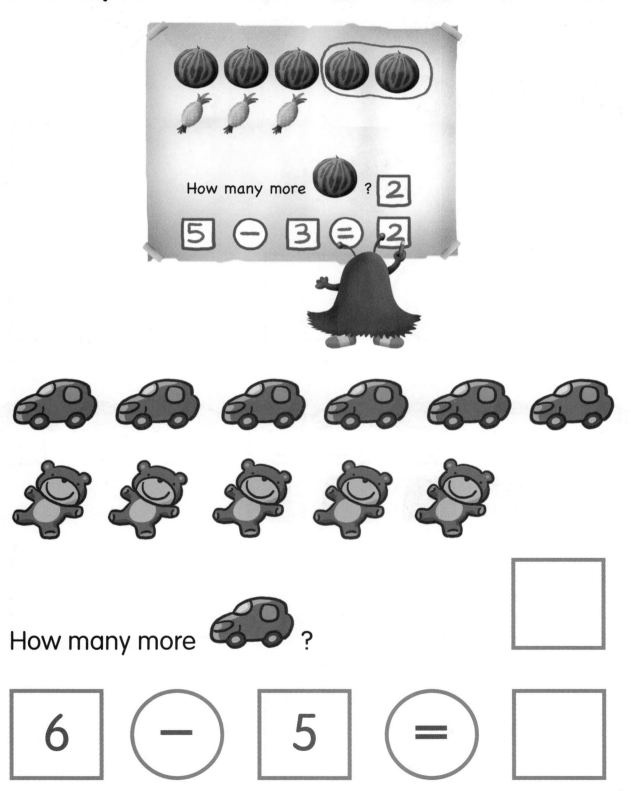

How many more 🚗 ?

6 (−) 5 (=)

How many more? Circle. Write the number sentence.

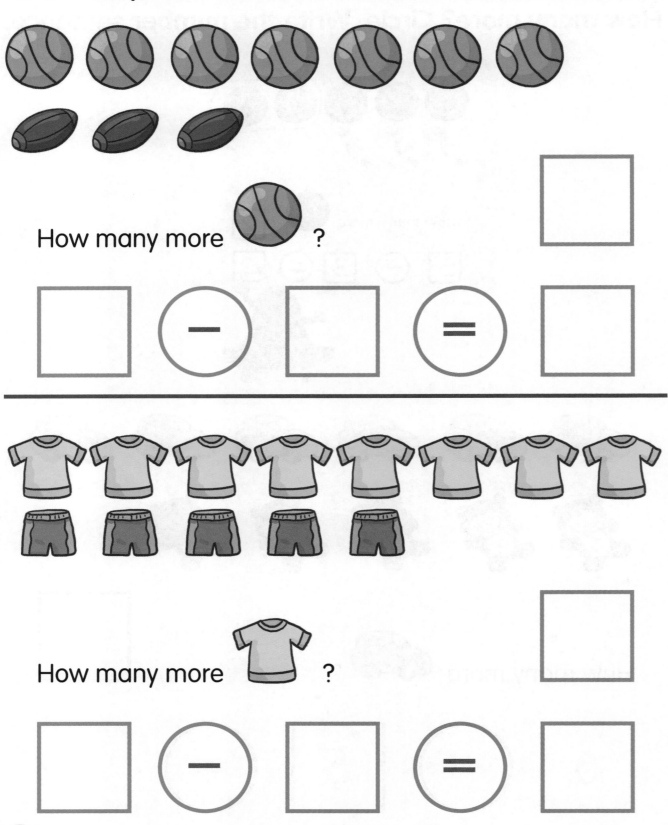

How many more 🏀 ?

☐ ⊖ ☐ ⊜ ☐

How many more 👕 ?

☐ ⊖ ☐ ⊜ ☐

How many more ?

How many more ?

How many more? Write the number sentence.

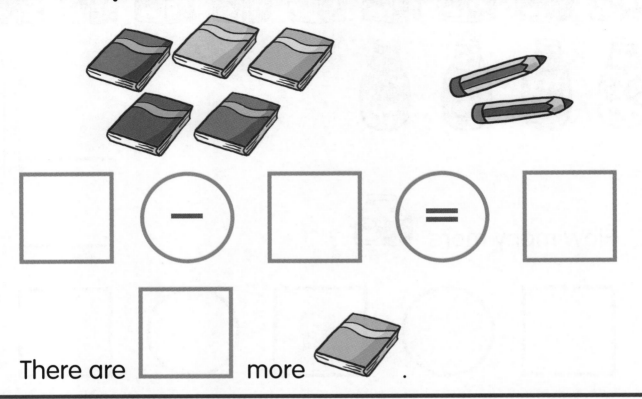

There are ☐ more 📗 .

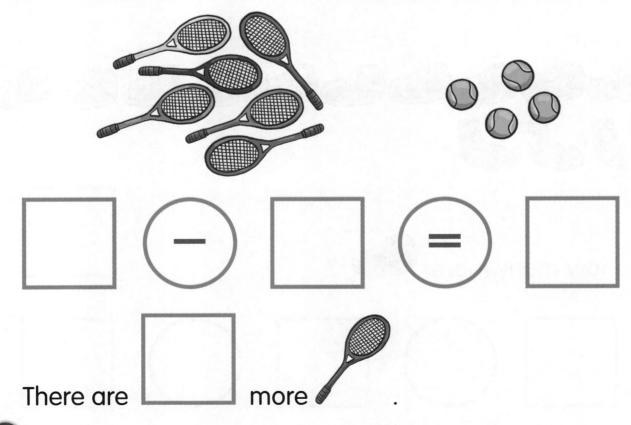

There are ☐ more 🎾 .

 —  = ◻

There are ◻ more  .

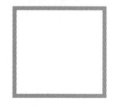 —  =

There are ◻ more  .

Measurement

Lesson 1 Comparing Weights Using Non-standard Units

Circle the heavier thing.

Circle the lighter thing.

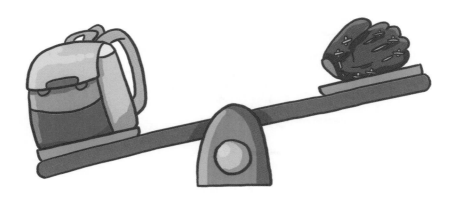

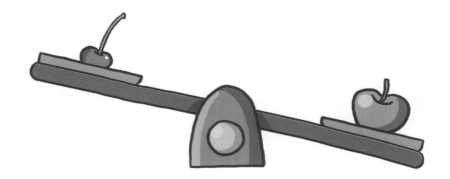

Count and write.

The owl weighs ☐ 🧱.

The mouse weighs ☐ 🧱.

Circle the heavier animal.

Count and write.

The teddy bear weighs 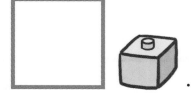 .

The doll weighs 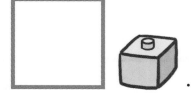 .

Circle the lighter thing.

Circle the container that holds more.

Circle the container that holds less.

Color the containers that hold the same amount.

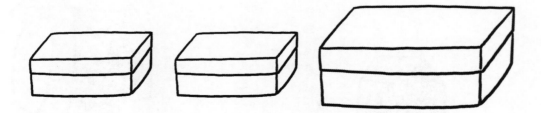

Lesson 3 Comparing Events in Time

Which takes more time? Circle.

Which takes less time? Circle.

Lesson 4 Comparing Areas Using Non-standard Units

How many squares will cover each thing?
Circle the bigger thing.

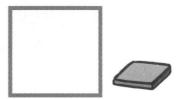

How many squares will cover each thing? Circle the smaller thing.

Lesson 1 Coin Values

Match.

   •   • 5¢

   •   • 25¢

     •   • 1¢

   •   • 10¢

How many pennies do you need? Color.

   and

 3¢

and  5¢

 2¢

and  4¢

and  3¢

How much is needed? Circle the purse.

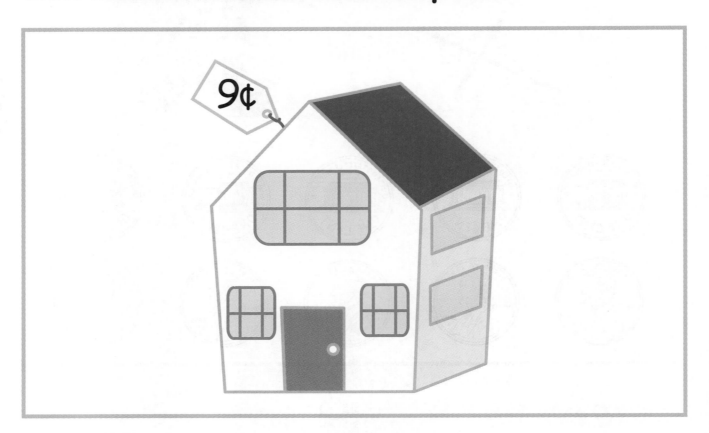

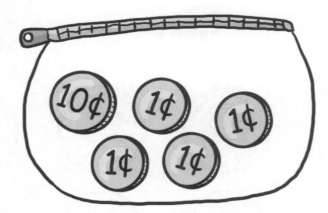

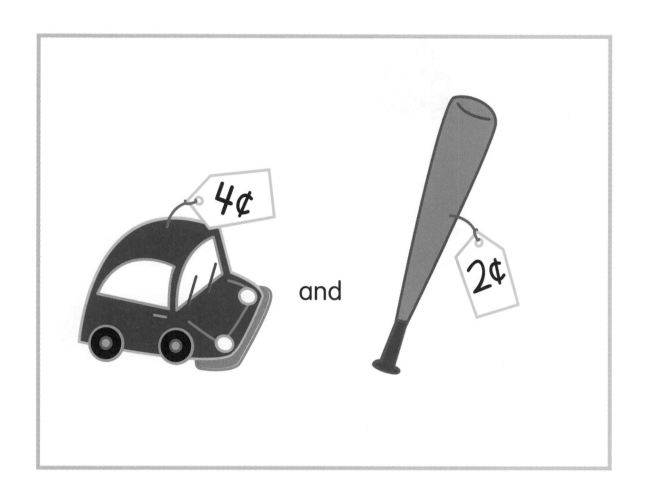

and

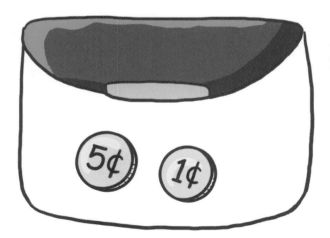